1

This book is a follow-up to *Becoming Free Through Meditation*, which was first printed for distribution to prisoners in 1992. In 1995 this book was expanded to include guidelines on yoga, so that both elements of the Trust's work are represented.

We have made free use of the words of Ruben Habito, Anthony de Mello, Henry Rennox, Swami Satyananda Saraswati, of countless prisoners and of many people who have been working with us at the Trust on behalf of prisoners. We express our gratitude to the many other friends of the Prison Phoenix Trust, who remain nameless.

There are other resources available from the Prison Phoenix Trust, including two CDs, a book for those who find reading difficult, one for those who can't read at all and a booklet for pregnant prisoners. Please get in touch to find out more about how we can help.

Published in 1995 by The Prison Phoenix Trust and reprinted in 1999, 2002, 2004, 2006, 2008, 2014 and 2016.

A CIP catalogue record for this book is available from the British Library.

ISBN 978-0-9550334-2-1

Printed by Berforts Limited, Hastings, East Sussex

Front cover: *Sun Rise*, from the London CRC Probation Service, winner of the Monument Trust Scholarship 2014 and Bronze Award for Painting. Picture provided by the Koestler Trust.

Contents

Becoming Free
through Yoga

By Sandy Chubb

Sandy leading a yoga session on the prison ship HMP The Weare

The Strip Cell

In the strip I sat
Humiliated, dejected, depressed.
It seems that no-one cares. Do they?
Well it seems not. Am I forgotten?

I hear a jangle of keys.
I bang, I shout, I swear,
It seems as there's no one there.
  Is there?
At last someone comes, my Saviour
  from this hell - or not.

What do I want?
The screw shouts at me.
'Just a chat, Guv' I say meekly.
'Not a chance lad,' he grunts.
Is this real or an illusion?
Who knows or cares?

Being Free through Yoga

Artist and former prisoner Peter Cameron says: *"The most enlightening and refreshing times I ever had in prison were in the yoga classes at HMP Full Sutton."*

Yoga could have been designed especially for prisoners when it came into being in India 5000 years ago. The very word means 'experiencing oneness' which happens when you allow the duality of mind and body to dissolve, realising a oneness with Creation. This 'taste' of the discipline of yoga is specially written for people serving time.

"I'm stressed out and I can't get my head together." That's the most common thing you tell us when we go to prisons up and down the country.

How can any of us get our heads together when our bodies are full of physical tension? When we sleep badly because the head keeps racing, and the body gets more and more wound up?

Many of you who are doing time in prisons where you can work out with weights or do gym find that this only partly helps. If you really want to find some peace, prisoners and non-prisoners will testify that the practice of yoga is an answer.

Asanas, or yoga postures, are held for a number of seconds so that you learn to stay steady, calm, quiet and comfortable. By stretching the muscles in a gentle way, you massage the internal organs and tone the nerves all over your body. Not only will you improve your health, but diseases can be improved and sometimes cured, with regular practice. You experience what Oneness is – perhaps for the first time.

What can yoga do for you in prison? Before he was released from HMP Springhill in 1995, Henry Rennox posed for the photographs in this book for us and, on page 60, says what yoga did for him. If you decide to give some of the following practices a try, you'll come up with your own answer. Yoga frees us – not just of our tensions and stress but of all the "stuff" we collect along the way which seems to stick like glue.

If you read the four newsletters a year the Prison Phoenix Trust sends to prisoners, you'll know the depth of our love for you. This book comes to you with more of the same.

Sandy Chubb

Asanas are unique

By exercising slowly, learning to consciously relax in each posture, and concentrating on the breath, both the external and internal systems are influenced. When you tune into the breath in this focused way, for periods of stillness, the practice of yoga begins. Everything starts to work properly from the glands to the nervous system ... to yourself.

So asanas don't just work on the body. When the mind is concentrated, power is released to work on infirmities because our bodies influence our minds. Something much deeper starts to happen too when your being dissolves into a harmony of breath, mind, body and spirit. You realise your Oneness. And without having to do a thing, without having to imagine anything or visualise anything, you experience the inner force – the Sacred – which is greater than your everyday self.

Tuning out … and tuning in

Funnily enough, it is this tuning out of the racket of your everyday lives and tuning in, with full concentration, into your inner being which many of you say you find so scary.

Ask you to fight an enemy, rescue a child from a burning house or climb a mountain and there's no problem. Ask instead that you release all your daily problems and clutter — even for as short a time as half an hour — and some of you say you feel unsafe. This kind of unknown can be a real challenge, maybe because you are connecting yourself with your mind which often causes unhappiness.

Nevertheless, yoga is the experience of unity with the body, mind and spirit. When you experience that union and, in turn realise that you are one with the rest of Creation, you can see that there is no need to be afraid. Because the mind, in this context, is just a tiny speck in a much greater whole. And how refreshed we feel after half an hour's practice like this.

Yoga can be practised by both healthy and unhealthy people, stiff and supple, young and old. It is a huge help for concentration and meditation.

***

Indian prisoner and yoga teacher Sri Aurobindo was wrongly arrested for terrorism and, in Alipore Jail, South of Calcutta, he was put in a stone cell, five feet long by five feet wide — a cave fronted by bars.

"At Alipore, I could feel how deep can be the love of man for all created things, how thrilled a man can be on seeing a bird. I looked instead towards a blank wall. Day after day, the mind rebelled and felt increasingly desolated, time itself an unbearable torture."

Then during his meditation practice, he discovered that yoga is not the product of personal effort. Acknowledging the existence of an inner force, he came to see a spirit of faith or reverence, and complete self-surrender, as the only route to wisdom and faith.

"Finally, there spread over my being, such a gentle and cooling breeze, the heated brain became relaxed, easy and supremely blissful, such as in all my life I had never known before. From that day, all my troubles of prison life were over."

Aren't weights enough?

"Physical exercises are performed quickly with a lot of heavy breathing ... Weight-lifting is suitable for healthy people to develop large muscles or flexibility. Very large muscles require more nutrition and a greater supply of blood and the heart and respiratory system have to work harder. In this way there is exhaustion of vital energy," says Swami Satyananda, who was an internationally respected yoga teacher.

There is nothing wrong with doing weights, when you do it properly, regularly and you are fit. It's even better if you integrate it with yoga to stretch out muscles which might have become foreshortened through strong contractions. But even if you are young, if you stop weight-training for a month or more, fat accumulates in place of the bulging muscles. If you are not young and fit, weights can't help you. Nor do they relax and rejuvenate in the way prisoners need. While we are on the subject, here's another difference too.

Weights are ego-strengthening and yoga is ego-releasing.

Hang on, my problem is...

1.   "I can't sit still for two seconds, let alone twenty minutes…"

You would be surprised how quickly time passes, when you are concentrating with your entire attention, on your breath — its sound, its length and its capacity.

Asanas are the key to learning how to maximise vital energy to be more effective. Instead of frittering away precious time and vitality, you learn to re-direct it so that it has maximum force only where and when it is needed. You'll find that you **can** sit quiet for long periods of calm because you'll see that the limitless potential for stillness is already within you.

2. "Yoga is for weirdos, women and wimps..."

The practice of yoga asanas evolved when people, not very different from prisoners, lived frugally many centuries ago. Their food was meagre, they had few medicines and their shelter was crude in the extreme.

Does that ring a bell with you in prison? They chose to live like this as part of their exploration into the essential world, but they knew they needed help to maintain themselves in healthy condition. For hundreds of years only men practised yoga, but gradually, householders learning of its benefits, adopted it too, along with their families.

In the last few decades, many of the secrets known to those ancient pioneers have been used by teaching hospitals, particularly for asthma, respiratory diseases, prostate, stress incontinence and back problems.

A study by Oxford University recorded that one simple half an hour programme increased people's energy by ten per cent. If you don't think yoga is very macho, you could be right, but guess which institution introduced yoga into this country in the nineteen thirties? The British Army!

People who do yoga include most professional athletes (most notably Ryan Giggs), actors like Orlando Bloom and Robert Downey Jr, musicians like Adam Levine and Jon Bon Jovi - and countless prisoners.

Many men who have spent long periods down the block in some tough institutions say that all the energy they put into violence is really a sort of self-protection. When you learn to conserve it, and find a peaceful balance in yourself, a curious thing takes place. Not only do you become more powerful as a person, because you are charging healthily, but this self-improvement leads into a calmer, happier and more sociable way of life.

Far from being regarded as a wimp, the increased self-respect you have for yourself, is echoed by everyone else around you.

But find this out for yourself ...

3. "I'm a dope user, heavy smoker and I'm pretty stiff. I never stick at anything..."

Right now you need to change one thing — which is the picture of yourself you hold up in front of your mind everyday. One of the reasons some people get sick is because they can never visualise themselves as well people.

So you don't need to do anything to yourself, you don't need to stop any habit, or face anything painful. When you are doing yoga, picture yourself well and happy.

People do yoga because it makes you feel good. Try it — just for a month. However stiff you are, if you practise gently, you'll become supple. Most smokers doing yoga, drop the habit. You needn't say to yourself that you need to give up cigarettes. Eventually, they give you up.

4. "I'm in a small cell and there's no room..."

Most yoga mats are two feet two inches by six feet. That's all the space you need to work on. You don't need a mat by the way, just a slip-free surface.

5. "I'm a Christian so I can't do a different religion..."

Because yoga isn't a religion it can be practised by anyone of any faith, or of none at all. It's a spiritual practice. In its advanced form it leads to a realisation of who we truly are.

The asanas and breathing techniques, concentration and meditation can help you deepen your faith, whatever it is, or open a door to fertile land which you may be unaware of.

Yoga began in India, the home of Hinduism and Buddhism. Yoga techniques have been used by other religious schools in India and worldwide, including in Christianity. See page 93.

How do I start ?

There are no better words than these of *The Upanishads* (which represents for the Hindu, what the New Testament does for the Christian) to describe the best way to do yoga. The earliest of these spiritual texts were put down about 800 BC ...

"And when the body is in silent steadiness, breathe rhythmically through the nostrils with a peaceful ebbing and flowing of breath. The chariot of the mind is drawn by wild horses, and those wild horses have to be tamed.

"Find a quiet retreat for the practice of Yoga, sheltered from the wind, level and clean, free from rubbish, smouldering fires, and ugliness, and where the sound of waters and the beauty of the place help thought and contemplation."

Prisons aren't the most lovely places but still you can practise beautifully wherever you are doing time. There are a few things which can help. Check your small floor area is clean and if it is possible, get in some fresh air by opening a window so that you can change the air in your lungs and purify the cells in your body. If there isn't a window, grab the chance to breathe deeply when you are allowed outside. If you are a smoker, clean the ashtray.

In your cell, you can remind yourself about nature by bringing in a leaf, twig or a stone from outside. If you have a window, look outside and tune into the clouds and sky before you begin. If you want to make a little ritual everyday before you start, (and you are allowed to) you can light an incense stick. If you are in a freer institution, you might also be allowed to light a candle. This ritual will help to leave the prison world behind while you enter the essential world. The leaf (or flower) reminds us that our bodies too will fade; the incense is to purify us and the candle is to give us illumination — to remind us of the Sacred within us that can never be destroyed, but only revealed.

What Time Of Day Is Best ?

In the morning, when the mind is clearest there is nothing so fine as yoga practice — particularly if it is followed by meditation. It gives the entire day a fresh appeal. When you first get out of bed, you need to work gently until the body loses the stiffness of the night. Greeting the rest of the day with a radiantly free body, and clear, peaceful mind is worth overcoming the stubbornness of the initial stiffness.

If you feel like it you can repeat some yoga in the evening when your body is at its most supple. It is good to become aware of the differences inside ourselves, at different times of the day and start accepting them without judgement.

The breath

In the West we know we have to depend on breath for Life. That is no problem for most of us. In the Orient there is a further revelation. For centuries, yoga teachers have taught that our mental power, happiness, self-control, clear-sightedness, morals and even our spiritual growth can be increased by understanding and using the breath to the full. Wow!

The Old Testament, Genesis 2.7 says, *"Then the Lord God formed man out of dust from the ground and breathed into his nostrils the breath of life and man became a living being."*

So the breath is SACRED.

A prisoner from HMP Stradishall says: *"Getting in touch with my breath, opened a new world for me, even in this place."*

So what is this mystery of the breath? The most important thing is to learn to breathe through the nose and overcome the common practice of mouth-breathing. Although it is possible to breathe through both nose and mouth, nose-breathing makes you healthier and stronger.

The nose is a brilliant piece of engineering designed to give us the highest quality breaths. It contains little filters to trap all the germs and dirt, and it warms and moistens the air on its journey to the delicate lining of the throat and lungs.

The normal rate of breathing is about 15 times a minute …

If a lot of technical stuff about the body bores you to death, then just skip over it. I put it in because so many prisoners seem to be interested in what is underneath the bonnet, so to speak.

So if you are interested in stripping down the engine, we have twelve ribs, able to move by connecting muscles, on each side which protect two lungs. As air comes into the nose, the muscles of the lungs (and ribs) expand and a vacuum is created to draw the air down. So that the lungs have space to fill, the diaphragm, which is a large dome shaped muscle separating the chest from the belly, automatically moves down.

Air percolates the lungs carrying oxygen into the bloodstream which flows into the heart. From there it circulates and nourishes every cell in the body. While all this is going on, waste products like carbon dioxide are thrown out by the lungs. As the diaphragm moves up, the lungs contract exhaling the waste products.

People think that because breathing is usually automatic, it is beyond their active control. This is not true.

Yoga teaches us ways to train the lungs and nervous system - to make breathing more efficient by changing its rate, depth and quality. The lung capacity of great athletes, mountain climbers and yogis is far greater than most people. Although during our daily life we breathe automatically - thank goodness! - we can lead better and healthier lives if we spend a period each day developing our breathing capacity.

The rate of yoga breaths a minute is about three or four.

Pranayama

Prana simply means the vital force which pervades all things. Breathing practice in yoga is called Pranayama.

The complete yoga breath

You can't do this all at once. When you start to play around with your breathing, testing out a more conscious way to breathe, you need to be patient and sensible. Try a little part of some of the instructions, explore how you feel and then breathe easily. Then you can try a bit more ...

Remember, all you are doing is breathing naturally and normally. If you want to examine how it all works (just like pulling apart the carburettor or checking the oil) then you can now look at it in more detail. But basically, it is just breathing — a little more slowly, a little more deeply. Stand or sit with the spine straight and the chin level.

1. Breathing through the nostrils, inhale steadily, first filling the lower part of the lungs, feeling how the diaphragm descends to bring a gentle pressure on the abdominal organs.

2. Then fill the middle part of the lungs, pushing out the lower ribs, breast-bone and chest.

3. Then fill the higher portion of the lungs, protruding slightly the upper chest, so that you are conscious that you have slightly lifted the chest including the upper six or seven pairs of ribs.

4. Retain the breath a second or two (yoga calls this the full vessel — it's a most important hold).

5. Breathe out quite slowly, just watching that your chest is being held in quite a firm position naturally as it draws the belly in a little and lifts it upward slowly as the air leaves the lungs. When the air is entirely exhaled, relax the chest and abdomen.

In the third step, the lower part of the abdomen or belly, will be slightly drawn in, which gives the lungs a support and also helps to fill the highest part of the lungs.

Trying this breath out from a book all at once can make you feel like a balloon

17

about to burst. That really isn't the idea. The complete yoga breath is just normal breathing looked at, if you like, under a microscope.

At first this might seem as though you are doing five different movements but really it is one continuous, steady breath. Practice will overcome any divisions and let you unite your breathing uniformly. There should never be any sense of strain. Don't try and fill your lungs to their absolute capacity. Eighty per cent is just fine.

Notice that there is a pause at the end of the breath when you are empty of air. This is a natural phenomenon. It is only by keen observation that you discover this subtle pause. There is no need to snatch at the next in-coming breath, or to rush to breathe in. Sometimes the pause is several seconds long. Your body is designed to inhale automatically. The pause at the end of the exhalation breath is something you can explore and let happen of its own accord. A little practice will make this an easy, almost automatic exercise.

Oddly enough, we don't really have a problem with breathing in. That just happens. But if we are upset in any way, sometimes we forget to breathe out and the breath can be held for quite long periods. That lets tension build up. The very act of breathing out is a letting go. It's a release, an expulsion of all the stuff we are bombarded with during a day, from news bulletins to ever-increasing information. When we learn the value of the exhalation breath our daily lives are transformed.

Magic cure

The complete yoga breath is truly magical. If you practise it for half an hour while you are doing asanas, or just practise it sitting still, you feel calmer, banish colds, and other diseases, rest the heart, improve your circulation and help prevent constipation. But don't take my word for it — try it for yourself and see.

There are lots of different breathing techniques in yoga. The complete yoga breath is the most basic — and the finest.

Asanas

Prisoners in regular classes are sometimes reluctant to take off their socks and trainers because they are worried their feet smell. All feet smell. Mine do. Once you can accept that, you can forget it. Feet need to be bare to be truly grounded. Practising with bare feet is better because it feels freer and safer since there is no danger from slipping. When the soles of the feet touch the floor with awareness, conscious of temperature and texture of the floor covering, and in tune with the subtle vibrations of the earth beneath them, you can find your proper balance.

How long should I hold each posture ?

An asana is a still posture or pose. Beginners can hold poses for twenty seconds, which is about three complete easy yoga breaths. While you are doing the pose, try not to breathe faster so that you can speed up the end of the hold. It is this still hold which has such transforming effects. Yoga teacher and one-time prisoner, Sri Aurobindo says : *"The first object of immobility of the asana is to get rid of the restlessness imposed on the body and to force it to hold the Pranic energy instead of dissipating and squandering it.*

"The body, accustomed to work off superfluous energy by movement, is at first ill able to bear this increase and this retained inner action and betrays it by violent tremblings; afterwards it habituates itself and, when the asana is conquered, then it finds as much ease in the posture ... as in its easiest attitudes, sedentary or recumbent."

Asanas help both your restless mind and restless body to become tranquil. If you find yourself breathing faster, go deeper into your concentration on the breath and just see if you can't relax into a slightly longer breath.

Asanas are best performed with an empty bladder, bowels and an empty stomach. That is why dawn is best, or at least three or four hours after eating. There should never be any sense of strain; even though your muscles at first will feel stiff and unbending, your body responds rapidly to regular practice and you will soon become more supple.

Precautions

Shoulderstand should be avoided if you have:

- High blood pressure
- A heart condition
- Gas or fermentation in the intestines
- A blood disorder
- A menstrual period
- Certain blood thinning drugs you take as medication (you will need to check with your doctor)
- Hiatus hernia
- Detached retina and glaucoma
- Neck injuries
- Certain back problems

Some prisoners don't feel comfortable talking to prison doctors. If you are one of them, maybe you won't know whether to practise a certain position or not. You can write to us at the Prison Phoenix Trust for more personal advice, but we are not medically qualified to help you. If you have some physical problem, please see your prison doctor.

When doing the asanas, always try to move slowly and with full awareness of your body. If you feel pain or pleasure, try not to react to it, but just observe. In this way you can develop powers of concentration and endurance. If you move to the point of pain, stop. Listen to your body. Don't stay in an asana if there is excessive discomfort.

You are your own best teacher although you may not yet be aware of it. By daily yoga practice you will become so familiar with your being, that you will learn to listen to its needs, its vibrations and you will discover how best to heal yourself.

Wear comfortable loose clothing — not jeans! Denim is too rigid to allow the body to stretch. When you start practising, be warm so that your muscles are protected. You can always peel off a sweater if you need to. Finally, again bare feet are best (that goes for meditation too).

Corpse pose

How strange to begin with a pose which means death instead of birth! But corpse pose is an ideal way for us to quieten and relax the body, to begin our practice.

Lie flat on your back with your arms at diagonals to the body. Your hands are a foot away from the hips, palms facing upwards drawing your shoulders away from your ears.

Check that your body is in a straight line, with your head straight and the chin tucked slightly downwards. Lift the pubic bone to tuck your buttocks under so there is no compression in the lower back. Relax. Let your feet fall apart either side of an imaginary central line, fully relaxing your hips, legs and feet.

Close your eyes gently and resolve to yourself not to move at all, even if some discomfort occurs. This is the pose of stillness where we learn true relaxation.

Let the breath be rhythmic and natural and stay alert to the inhalation and exhalation. Focus the mind attentively on the breath at all times, mentally counting each out-breath until you reach ten, when you begin again.

If the mind isn't absorbed in concentrated breath focus, you become drowsy and the asana weakens into just lying on the floor. At the start and end of the asana programme you can hold this pose for five minutes. If you want to increase the length of the practice, so much the better. It is a very helpful asana to do at night if you want a good night's sleep.

A life prisoner at HMP Kingston took a yoga teachers' training while he was doing time. *"The worst thing about practising my yoga has been the disturbance from other people when I am doing the relaxation pose. But you find a way to overcome that."*

"The path of Yoga is not easy, every inch of ground has to be won against much resistance. The aspirant must be patient and firm to face difficulties, and obstacles of all sorts with a calm and serene spirit."

~ *S. R. Tiwari*

Yoga spills over into your everyday life. When you are more aware of your body you can find out how to release it when it gets tense. By understanding the calming effects of the breath, you can take the heat out of a fiery situation by staying centred. That very tranquillity has an effect on other people. Another interesting thing happens when you see that how you present yourself to other people, your appearance that is, is what they see. For instance, an upright posture looks and feels confident. Cared-for hair, cleanliness and a relaxed expression suggests a person who is in control of themselves. Others recognise that in you and respond to it.

When you discover how warmed you feel by someone else's smile when they say hello, you learn to smile too. Learning to smile genuinely is the single most difficult and most important thing for many of us to remember. And it brings the greatest rewards. So yoga can go on helping you in the smallest, most ordinary things. Many of you with some knowledge of yoga often ask about aspects like diet and special practices. The following quote gives a perfect guideline.

"Extremes should be avoided: too much fasting or too little sleep weakens the body and is detrimental to the nervous system. If we practise moderation and discipline, balance our eating and sleeping habits along with our work and time we spend awake, we shall reach perfect harmony with the Self. In this way Yoga banishes pain and misery. To achieve this perfect harmony and complete equilibrium, we must have absolute control of both mind and body."

~ *S. R. Tiwari*

Wind-releasing pose

This pose massages the abdomen and helps remove wind and constipation.

Lie flat on your back, bend your right leg and bring your right thigh near the chest. Interlock your fingers and place them over the right knee. Inhale deeply and exhale. In the pause while you are empty of breath, lift your head and upper portion of the chest and try to touch your right knee with your nose. Then inhale and return the head to the floor. Relax. Repeat ten times with each leg.

Then fold both legs and wrap your arms around your knees. Repeat the head and upper chest-raising movement 10 times, taking care to co-ordinate the breath with the body movements.

Bridge pose

This is a good pose for anyone with general back problems as it strengthens and improves the back without any great strain. It is a powerful breathing aid too.

Lie on your back, bend your knees, place your feet hip distance apart on the floor, parallel to each other with your heels close to your bottom. Your arms lie alongside your trunk palms downwards.

1. Inhale and retain your breath for a few seconds. As you slowly exhale, squeeze your buttock muscles, and pressing the back of your waist into the ground, lift your pubic bone so that the pelvis is tilted upwards. Enjoy the long pause of emptiness while you wait for your body to breathe in, in its own time.

2. As your breath comes into the nostrils for the inhalation, peel the entire back off the floor, lifting your arms behind you and your hips high towards the ceiling, squeezing your buttock muscles and lengthening your lower back. Pause full of breath.

3. Stay in that position while you exhale slowly, contracting the muscles between the shoulder blades, lifting your chest slightly higher and relaxing your neck and shoulder-joint muscles. Pause empty of breath. When you are ready, deeply inhale. Pause.

4. As you exhale, lower your back down slowly on the floor, bone by bone, trying to get your waist vertebra on the floor before you lengthen out the lower back bringing your arms back down to your sides. Pause and wait for the inhalation while you enjoy relaxing. You can repeat this movement six times.

Floor twist

Floor twists help relieve lower-back aches, bring flexibility to the spine, stretch the abdominal muscles and stimulate proper action of the digestive and eliminative systems.

Lie on your back with your knees on your chest. Inhale deeply and as you exhale, still in the curled up position, roll over onto your right side as you would on your bed at night. Relax completely. In this curled up, foetal position, stretch your arms out in front along the floor with the left arm on top. Inhale, keep your eyes on your left arm as you lift it towards the ceiling. Exhaling, take the left arm down to your left side, opening your chest and shoulders until the left arm is at shoulder height, lying outstretched and resting on the ground. Turn your head and look along your left arm to the left (see picture 1). You can feel your hips pointing one way and your ribcage is moving to the other. Gradually, your shoulders become more flexible as they loosen up and learn to relax your left shoulder down onto the ground.

Breathe deeply into your left lung for three breaths. At first that may seem impossible. Visualise your breath going into the left lung and keep your mind on what you are doing. With the mind and imagination working with the body, you will discover how this can happen. Roll onto your back, centre yourself, and repeat on the other side (see picture 2).

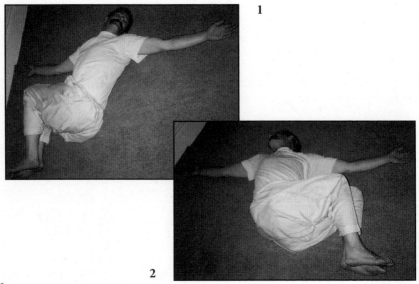

1

2

Cobblers pose

This is how cobblers sit in India and is a good pose for people with tight hip joints, as it loosens the hipsockets, stretches the inner-thigh muscles, and yet it does not place stress upon the knee-joints.

Sit upright and bring the soles of your feet together, pull your heels as close to your groin as possible, interlace the fingers, and clasp your hands around your toes. Using your feet for leverage, lift your chest forward, straighten your spine and release your knees towards the floor. Continue working in the pose for 20 seconds, building up to two minutes, breathing deeply.

"The most beautiful and most profound emotion we can experience is the sensation of the mystical. It is the source of all true science. He to whom this emotion is a stranger, who can no longer wonder and stand rapt in awe, is as good as dead.

To know that what is impenetrable to us really exists manifesting itself as the highest wisdom and the most radiant beauty which our dull faculties can comprehend only in their most primitive forms – this knowledge, this feeling is at the centre of true religiousness."

From *The Universe and Dr Einstein* by Albert Einstein

"Are you looking for me? I am in the next seat.
When you really look for me, you will see me instantly —
You will find me in the tiniest house of time.
Kabir says: Student, tell me, what is God?
He is the breath inside the breath."

Kabir

Frog pose

This asana is wonderful because we don't have to struggle against gravity to hold the pose. Instead, the floor becomes our friend. The asana opens your hips, frees the groins — which greatly aids freedom from lower back-problems — opens your chest and stimulates deep breathing. Like cobblers pose, it helps us prepare for sitting meditation.

Kneel upright with your knees apart as far as is comfortable, allowing your big toes of your feet which are flat on the floor to barely touch beneath your buttocks. Keeping your buttocks on the heels of your feet at all times, gradually lean forward until your hands touch the floor. Continue bending forwards until your arms are stretched along the floor, letting your chest and trunk sink down in front of you and your forehead touch the floor. Your ribs and chest are quite free and deep breathing can be practised with ease and fluency. At first in this position, your groins may feel tight and you may feel that three rhythmic yoga breaths is enough. If you bring your knees closer together it is more comfortable. As your groin becomes freer, you can keep your knees wider apart.

Cat pose

For bringing flexibility to the spine and stimulating the spinal fluid, the continuous wave-like spinal movement of cat asana has no equal. It releases excess tension in the digestive tract so that the food breakdown can occur more efficiently. It stimulates the digestive system to release necessary hormones for further food digestion, aids the eliminative system and greatly increases the efficiency of the nervous system.

Kneel, stretch forwards and put your hands on the floor. Come onto all fours on your hands and knees, with your hips directly above your knees (hip-width apart) and your shoulders above your hands. Your spine is horizontal and your eyes look down at the central spot on the floor between your thumbs.

Inhale. As you start to exhale, tuck your tail-bone under, contract your abdominal muscles pulling them back hard towards your spine, arch the back like an angry cat, and allow your chin to come towards your chest to squeeze out the last of the air from your lungs. (Here you are performing the chin and stomach locks (see page 56 and 58). When you become practised in this asana, you can add the pelvic lock as well at the end of the breath.)

After the pause at the end of the exhalation, as you feel air rushing in to fill the lungs, let your tail-bone turn up, hollowing your back, as your abdominal muscles drop passively towards the floor. Following the curve of the spine look up. Exhale, and repeat for six to ten rounds.

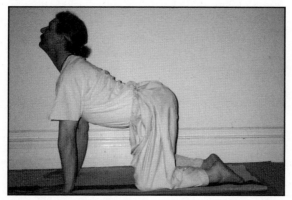

Mountain pose

Stand with the feet together. Bring your awareness to the soles of your feet. Get the feel of being balanced. (If you notice that you wear your shoes down on one side, you are probably standing unevenly now. Make sensitive shifts until your weight feels more balanced.) The weight should be equal on the triangles of your feet, from your big toes to the little toes, and from both to a point in the centre of your heels. Stabilise your ankles by slightly lifting the inner ankle bones and feel a drawing up movement in your legs as you contract your thigh muscles and gently lift your kneecaps. As your tail-bone tucks between your legs slightly, it decreases the curve in the small of the back. Draw back your belly muscles. The whole of your lower body will feel dynamic. Wide from side to side and flat from back to front. At this stage, your trunk and arms are still easy.

Now bring your attention to your chest, slightly raising your breast-bone and letting your shoulders drop back and down over the dome of your chest cage. The crown of your head moves up bringing your chin level, if anything very slightly down. Your eyes look down at a spot on the floor your body's length in front of you and automatically you feel your inner awareness watching the breath. Breathe deeply and rhythmically. A wonderful pose for improving posture, spirits and outlook.

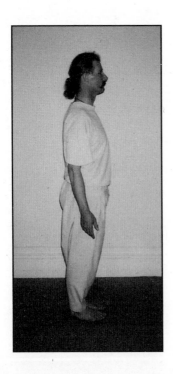 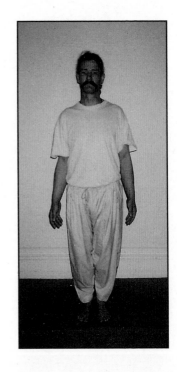

Moving mountain

Stand with the feet hip-width apart, your hands by the sides. As you breathe in deeply, raise your arms until your hands are over your head and you are full of breath. Retain the breath for a few seconds, then turn the palms of your hands outwards and in time with the out breath, lower your arms to your sides. Watch the pause at the end of the exhalation. Repeat five more times. You can come onto tiptoe as you raise the arms and keep your balance with the eye focus if you want to. This is a superlative pose to change the air in your lungs and wake up the body at the beginning of the day.

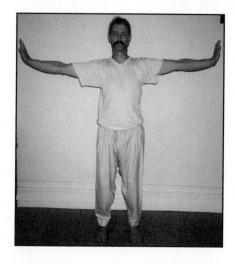 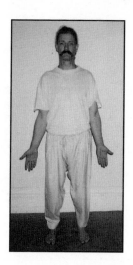

Triangle

This looks simple and feels difficult, especially at first. Its benefits are numerous since it develops the arches of the feet, strengthens the ankle joints, increases the circulation of the inner thighs by stretching them, strengthens the thigh, buttock and neck muscles, and improves digestion and elimination.

Place your feet about a metre apart (the width should be the same as your inside leg measurement). Turn your right foot out 90 degrees and turn the toes of your left foot in strongly. Lift the arches of both feet by grounding your big toes, lift your kneecaps and draw back the left hip to the wall behind you. Keeping your hips level and forward facing (although both feet are pointing to the right), centre your spine in an upright position, equally between both feet. Free your shoulders from tension if they have hunched up, inhale and raise your arms to shoulder height, extending your fingertips away from each other to fully open your shoulder joints. As you exhale, without letting your left hip collapse forward, extend your right arm to the right, feeling as though you are trying to stretch for something on a shelf just beyond you, all the time extending your right torso. Inhale in that position and fold in deeply in your right hip. Exhale and continue the bend over to the right, this time letting your right hand come down somewhere on the right leg, between the knee and the ankle, depending on your suppleness. Like a windmill, your left arm lifts and points up at the ceiling. Check that both legs stay straight and the knees do not bend. Inhale and the next time you exhale, turn your head and look up at the thumb of your upraised left hand.

Breathing deeply in the asana, allow your lower right side of the hip, buttock, and ribcage to move forwards and the upper left side to move backwards, as the left ribcage opens the chest. Stay in the pose for at least 20 seconds and repeat on the other side, as shown in the pictures.

Warrior

As the name implies, this pose needs courage, stamina and strength. This is the pose of the hero — but it is the hero who is a defender and protector, not an aggressor. Although this pose looks graceful, it takes a lot of work to maintain.

Warrior pose opens your hips to the utmost, develops the arches of the feet, tones the buttocks, thighs, and abdominal muscles, loosens the shoulder joints, increases the lung capacity by stretching the chest muscles and increases the circulation of blood throughout the body.

To begin, spread your feet, four feet apart (more if you are tall) and pigeon-toe the feet inwards. Then, without disturbing your left foot, turn your right foot out, as in the triangle pose. Bend your right knee until your right thigh is parallel to the floor and your right shin and calf are directly vertical over your right ankle. Your bent right leg forms a 90 degree angle. Don't let your right knee fall forwards or inwards over the right foot as this puts strain on the knee. Instead, keep taking it to the right as you further open your hips. Your back left leg stays straight and this is your anchor, your powerful steel girder which helps you maintain the pose. When your legs are in position, inhale and raise your arms to shoulder height, checking that they are exactly level and that your hands and wrists are working dynamically, in line with your arms. Your shoulders should be free of tension so try to direct the work in this part of your body to your arms and hands only.

When your arms are in position, turn your head and, keeping your chin level or if anything slightly down, look along your right arm letting your eyes focus, without hardening the gaze, on your middle fingernail. Your spine stays centred and erect. Direct your attention to the deep breath and maintain the pose for 20 seconds. Repeat on the other side.

South African life prisoner Nelson Mandela, who won the Nobel Peace Prize, said:

"I learned that courage was not the absence of fear but the triumph over it. The brave man is not he who does not feel afraid but he who conquers that fear.

As I walked out of the door towards the gate I knew if I didn't leave my bitterness and hatred behind, I'd still be in prison.

For to be free is not merely to cast off one's chains, but it is to live a way that respects and enhances the freedom of others."

Stretched Flank

This pose can follow naturally from the warrior pose. Maintain the warrior pose, then drop your arms and bend sideways to the right, sliding your right arm downwards so that your right hand touches the floor. Push your right arm back against the right knee. Now, open the chest by placing your left thumb at the base of the spine and as your left shoulder turns up to reach back to the wall behind you, look up. Release your left hand from its position on your back and stretch it up, then bring it to the right, at a diagonal angle over your left ear and head directly above your right leg. The palm of your left hand faces down but don't let your left arm collapse. It should be dynamic and feel as though it is stretching the entire left flank of your body upwards. If you can, work towards looking up in front of your upper left arm. Breathe deeply for 20 seconds and repeat on the other side.

Stretched flank pose reinforces all the benefits of warrior and lengthens your waist so there is more room for your internal organs to work better.

Tree balance

One of the gifts of the yoga balancing poses is that they can't be achieved unless your head — or mind — is together with your body. So when you are feeling fragmented, and all over the place, allow your breath to deepen and slow down and do mountain pose. See page 32. Relax into the pose and bring your attention to your left leg. Gradually move your weight in a very delicate way until you feel it is being borne by your left leg. Allow your right knee to bend and draw up your lower right leg until your right foot can be reached by your right hand. Guide the sole of your right foot onto the inner thigh of your left leg, tucking your right heel up high into your groin. Feel the contracting of your buttock muscles as you encourage your bent knee backwards and keep your hips facing squarely forwards. Your chin should be level, or slightly down, and you can breathe deeply and easily. Your eyes focus on a spot on the floor, your body's length in front of you, and this is a great help for your balance.

When your body is settled, raise your arms above the head and bring the palms of your hands together. Link your thumbs over each other and lifting through your inner standing leg, stretch up, bringing lightness and freedom to the pose. Hold the pose for at least 20 seconds and repeat on the other side. If at first you wobble, don't worry.

Until the body gets used to balancing, there are lots of easy options you can try first. You can either just place one foot on another, or place the foot of the bent leg on the inside calf of the standing leg or you can practice the pose by a wall, and hold onto the wall until you feel safe enough to stand on your own. Even the most unbalanced people find equilibrium in this pose so don't give up.

Shoulderstand

Shoulderstand is known as the queen of the asanas. The thyroid and parathyroid glands in the throat are directly stimulated in this pose because of the inverted position of the body, neck and head position. The thyroid gland controls the body's metabolic rate. Daily practice of the pose will help decrease headaches, nervousness, hypertension, insomnia and ulcers, as well as an improvement of memory and mental alertness (to name just a few of its rich gifts).

The shoulderstand must be approached with caution to avoid damage to the neck. A thickly-folded blanket to keep the weight off the neck is needed, and, in the first stages, a wall. The blanket should be 3 inches thick and folded so that it is wider than your shoulders and as long as your arms. You may need two blankets to get the right thickness.

It is important to place the shoulders on the blanket and take care to place the neck and head precisely on the floor or you will do more harm than good.

Lie on your back with your shoulders even in the centre of the blanket, about two inches from one of the blanket's edges. The base of your neck rests on the edge of the blanket but the back of your head should be on the floor. Your shoulders must be parallel to the edge of the blanket. If your shoulders shift so that they hang over the edge when you are coming up into shoulderstand, then come down and shift your position.

If you have never done anything like this pose before, place the blankets next to a wall and arrange yourself correctly on the blankets with your legs up the wall and your bottom closely touching the angle of the wall and the floor. Remember that the back of your head should rest on the floor with your shoulders evenly placed a couple of inches from the edge of the blanket.

1

2

3   4

Bend your knees, bring the soles of your feet to the wall, lift your bottom off the floor, See picture 2 page 43. Lift your hips and move your feet up the wall until your knees form a 90 degree angle. Tuck your pelvis under by squeezing your buttocks, push your arms down, bring the top of your chest to the chin, and let your neck muscles passively stretch out. See picture 3. The neck bones should not be on the floor. Work in this pose for 20 seconds, continuing to relax your ears, head, neck, throat and shoulders as much as possible.

Walk up the wall until your legs straighten. See picture 4. Work your thighs by lifting your front thigh muscles. To start with, stretch through your calves by bringing the toes away from the wall with your heels remaining on the wall. Eventually the toes are pointed in a relaxed manner. Tuck your pelvis by contracting your buttocks, and lift through your upper back. Make sure that your shoulders have remained on the blanket and the back of your head on the floor. Work for a further 20 seconds.

Then bend your elbows and place your hands on the back with your fingers pointing upwards. Keep your elbows as close together as possible, press your upper arms down, relax your neck muscles, lift up through your spine and work strongly through your buttocks and legs, holding the pose for a further 20 seconds.

5

As a beginner, you are just conscious of the work of the pose. The strangeness of being upside down with the head lower than the heart can make you feel tense. That's why it is important to keep pausing and relaxing all the time you are working in the pose. As you become more practised, you can take your feet off the wall and direct them overhead with the toes over your cheeks. See picture 5. You always strive to bring the chest to the chin, not the other way around, by walking the hands down towards the shoulder blades on the back. The key to the pose, believe it or not, is relaxation, and of course, the breath. When you have taken up the shape of shoulderstand, consciously relax as much of your throat, ears, neck and head as you can, by using the sound of the slow out-breath to calm the activity in your mind and body.

Come down from shoulderstand exerting the same control that you went into it with. Breathe and absorb the effects. Shoulderstand should not be performed immediately after an aerobic exercise — like the yoga sun salutes — when your heart rate is raised. Wait until your body feels calm.

Beginners can work towards holding the pose for a minute. When you become familiar with it, you can hold it for five to ten minutes. See page 20 before attempting this asana to check the precautions.

Dr Sheila Cassidy (a patron of the Prison Phoenix Trust), who was imprisoned and then tortured in Chile for her work with dissidents, says:

"When I was in prison, I was a great deal freer than my jailors. I used to write out Lovelace's poem for people … Stone walls do not a prison make, nor iron bars a cage … and those words of Romans 8: Death, nor life … nor height, nor depth, nor any other creature shall be able to separate us from the love of God…

"When I was in solitary confinement I found out that when I wanted to batter against the bars to be let out — like a child screaming to be let out — the understanding of God's will being done gave me acceptance and as soon as I was accepting of my situation, it was all right."

Fish pose

Fish pose is not only a perfect counter-pose for shoulderstand but it is wonderful for anyone with a rigid middle and upper back since it isolates these muscles and forces them to work. So if you have bad posture, your shoulders are slumped, and you need to improve your breathing, it is worth practising fish pose daily.

Lie on your back, stretch your legs straight and bring your elbows down by the lower part of your ribs making a soft fist of your hands. Then, as you inhale, keeping your bottom on the floor, arch your shoulder-blades and neck upwards as you tilt your head back so you can look at the wall behind you. There should be an even weight on your head, elbows, bottom, and heels. Your head should not take all the weight even though you are working towards bringing the top of your head to the floor. Contract strongly between your shoulder blades. Hold for 20 seconds breathing deeply and slowly and then allow your head to slide away as you relax back on the floor and absorb the effects of the asana.

A man is born gentle and weak.
At his death he is hard and stiff.
Green plants are tender and filled with sap.
At their death they are withered and dry.
Therefore the stiff and unbending is the disciple of death.
The gentle and yielding is the disciple of life.
Thus an army without flexibility never wins a battle.
A tree that is unbending is easily broken.
The hard and strong will fall.
The soft and weak will overcome.
From the *Tao Te Ching* by Lao Tzu

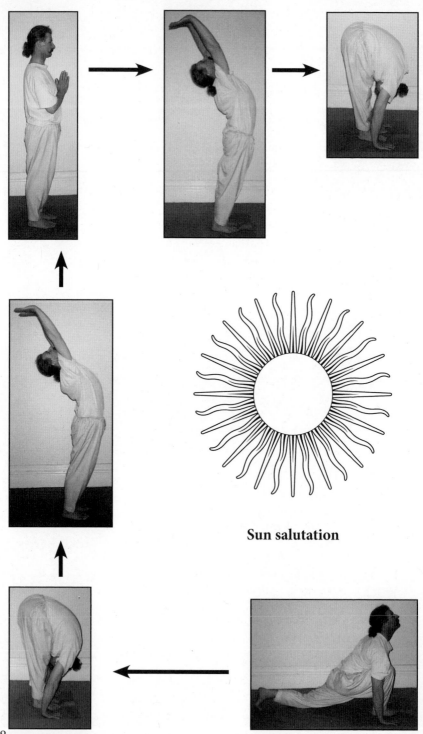

Sun salutation

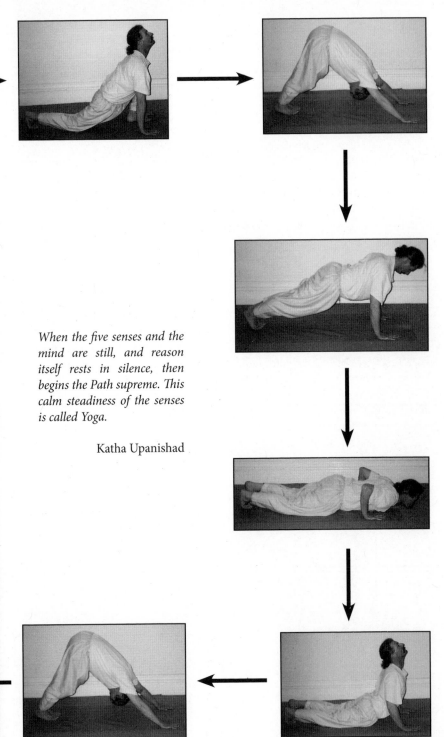

When the five senses and the mind are still, and reason itself rests in silence, then begins the Path supreme. This calm steadiness of the senses is called Yoga.

Katha Upanishad

49

Sun salutation

The beautiful sun salute sequence is your union with the whole of creation. It frees the light within your heart and the brilliance of the sun to radiate as one. The sun salutes are twelve poses which are performed once on the left side and once on the right side of the body repeated 12 times, linked together in a long, flowing motion. The movements loosen, energize and bring great harmony to your entire body. The important role of the autonomic nervous system in regulating our internal organs and systems is greatly helped by this practice. It is one of the most highly recommended sets of postures. It should be performed facing the sun as a moving meditation keeping the attention absorbed in the breath so make it a project to find out which way your cell faces if you can. The flow of arching up and bowing down allows you express reverence and gratitude to your union with the whole of creation – as well as to the sun's life-giving properties. When you practise the sun salutes, you are honouring your own divinity within the universe.

The sequence is traditionally performed in the morning to wake-up the body. Begin in an easy way, allowing for the stiffness of the night to disperse. That may take several movements. The sequence is often used as a warm-up for further yoga practice. Usually, the sun salutation is performed with one movement per breath. By both moving your body rhythmically and by flowing with your breath, you can get your body and your mind working in unison. It helps to balance the assertive and receptive parts of our being.

1. Mountain pose

Mountain pose with your hands in prayer position at the heart centre. Inhale and exhale fully.

2. Upwards stretch

Inhale. Stretch your arms up. With soft knees, and tail-bone tucked under, exhale as you arch your arms and body backwards. Inhale and straighten, pointing your fingertips to the ceiling.

3. Forward bend

Exhaling, bend forward and touch the floor next to your feet. At first your legs will feel tight at the back and you may need to bend your knees but with practice you'll be able to keep your legs straight. Your head should hang down relaxed off your neck.

4. Equestrian pose

Exhaling, extend your right leg back resting your right knee on the floor as you bend your left knee and bring your hands down to either side of your left foot.

Inhaling, lean your head back and look up.

5. Dog pose

Exhaling, taking your left foot back to stand alongside your right foot, raise up your bottom to the ceiling and stretch through your hands and arms. Your head drops down between your shoulders. Stretch your chest back to your thighs, forming a triangle shape with the floor. Inhale.

6. Plank pose

Exhaling, lower your bottom half-way down until your entire body is in a straight line with your shoulders over the hands. In the press-up position, lower your body to the floor. Keep your toes tucked under and your hands and elbows in the same position. Your forehead touches the floor. Inhale.

7. Cobra pose

As you exhale squeeze your buttocks and tuck your tail-bone under. Using your hands, raise your upper body using the strength in your arms to try to keep your shoulders from rising up around your ears. Inhale.

8. Dog pose

Exhale and return to dog pose by swinging your buttocks high to the ceiling. Inhale.

9. Equestrian pose

Exhaling, swing the right foot forward.

10. Forward bend

Exhale and draw up your left foot forward to join your right foot and raise your bottom in the forward bend.

11. Upwards stretch

Inhaling, raise your body upright and stretch your arms up above your head. Exhaling, bend backwards. Inhale and straighten, pointing fingertips to the ceiling.

12. Mountain pose

Exhale as you return your body to mountain pose. It's a good point to remind yourself of the profound meaning of the sequence you are practising.

Now repeat the movements with your left leg leading and you will then have completed one round (there are 24 movements in all). Round one is repeated eleven more times. You can decide on the pace for yourself, fast or slow. Feel free to breathe differently if you like according to your own rhythm. After the Sun Salutation relax in corpse pose for at least three minutes.

All of the sun salutes can be practised separately when you want to work on a particular part of the body. They can be incorporated into a daily programme which you can devise for yourself, using the 26 poses here, or any others you may know of.

You may have heard of the Blessed Mountain.
It is the highest mountain in our world.
Should you reach the summit you would have only one desire,
and that to descend and be with those who dwell in the deepest valley.
That is why it is called the Blessed Mountain.

Kahlil Gibran

The power of the internal locks

Usually, yoga locks are taught to more advanced students. But because they are such a powerful help in helping combat depression, mental strain, stress incontinence and prostate problems, and because prison is an ideal place in many ways — just like an ashram — to perfect the locks, as well as to enjoy the fruits of their benefits, the locks get a mention briefly here.

By locking or contracting certain muscles, a subtle process of 'unlocking' goes on at the same time simultaneously at mental and psychic levels. The locks have far reaching effects because they are associated with energy centres in the spine and brain. There are three locks.

1. Pelvic lock

Sit comfortably erect, relax completely, close your eyes, and focus your attention on the contact point between your chair or cushion and your perineum. What's the perineum? The perineum is the area at the base of your trunk between your legs. It stretches the length of the pelvic floor. With your mind, locate the central point between the anus and the scrotum, or clitoris. Don't worry about all the anatomical words. Let's hope they get clearer as you read on.

The pelvic lock doesn't mean contracting the whole perineum but the central point only for men, and for women, an area above the central point at the beginning of the cervix.

First, become intensely aware of the slight but distinct pressure at the outside central pressure point. Centre yourself at the pressure point.

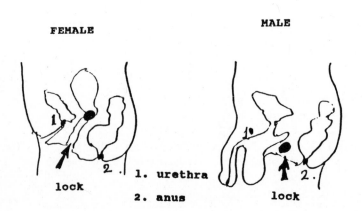

FEMALE   MALE

lock   1. urethra   2. anus   lock

56

Now, become aware of your natural breath, and imagine you are breathing in and out of the pressure point, for ten deep breaths.

Then bring your awareness inside the body by moving the pressure point up by contracting and pulling up everything between the legs to a central point three centimetres above the perineum. It may feel as though you are drawing your entire pelvic floor up towards your internal navel.

At first it seems that you are contracting the anal muscles and the muscles of the urethra — the muscle which controls the flow of urine. Don't worry. Regular practice of this lock will enable you eventually to refine and isolate just the muscles involved at the central point.

Like every other yoga practice, the key though, is moderation. Ten minutes daily with the complete yoga breath, holding the contraction for one breath is ample. Better still, split the time up into two five-minute practices.

2. Chin lock

The chin is locked when it is pressed down into the jugular notch, compressing the throat, stretching the neck, pulling the spinal cord and the brain.

You can lock the chin with a held breath or when you are empty of breath. The lock stimulates the thyroid glands and has beneficial mental and physical effects. You might like to practice it with the complete yoga breath for a short time, or a longer time but not more than ten minutes daily.

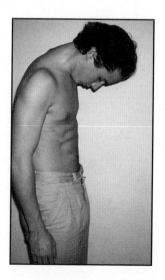 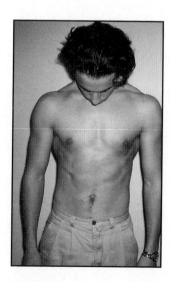

3. Stomach lock

This is an abdominal contraction compressing the digestive organs, adrenal glands, kidneys and the solar plexus. After these are squeezed by the contraction of the solar plexus muscles, a flood of internal energy is released, generating a sense of well-being. It is performed by standing easily upright, with the back slightly curved, the tail-bone tucking under and the legs a little wider than hip-width apart, with the knees slightly bent. Press hard on the thighs with the hands, inhaling. Exhale completely.

When you are empty of breath, in the pause at the end of the breath, contract and pull up the abdomen and stomach by drawing it back towards the spine, creating an empty cavity inside the ribs. Release when you need to breathe in. Then do the chin-lock to balance the energies.

This lock can only be performed when your stomach is empty of food so it is best practised in the morning before you do yoga asanas. To begin with, repeat the exercise three to five times, gradually increasing the number until it is possible to perform the asana at least twelve times if you wish.

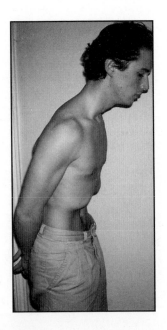 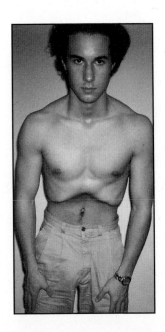

The locks and you

In a few weeks or months time, when you feel you have really mastered the three locks, you can gently explore how you can include them as one triple lock in your pranayama practice for a few minutes daily.

Since locks are taught usually by skilful teachers to well-practised yoga students, be skilful and cautious in your approach to them. Feel responsible for your precious body - it is the only one you have - and treat it kindly. Not everyone has a chance to go to a prison yoga class, and mastering a practice from a book is not the best method to learn. So here are some cautions to be aware of.

1. Don't let there be any sense of strain. If there is, stop.

2. If you are suffering from a heart ailment, high blood pressure, vertigo, high intercranial pressure or (women) lack of periods, then seek clearance with the prison doctor before practising the locks.

3. If you have any doubts or fears, just ignore the lock techniques, and move on instead to asana practice.

There are countless yoga books on different aspects of the practice if you want to learn more. A good general one is *Asana Pranayama Mudra Bandha* by Swami Satyananda Saraswati, published by Bihar School of Yoga.

People sometimes say they can't change. In a few months, there is almost a complete change in the matter composing the body, and scarcely a single atom now composing your body will be found in it in a few months time. We change all the time. Daily yoga practice helps people change for the better.

We often think we can't change because all of us know what it is like trying to improve ourselves, then failing. Just depending on the will doesn't seem to be enough. When we surrender our will to our Sacred power and let that be the chief operating agent, this is where the real healing begins. Yoga prepares the body beautifully for living to our fullest potential. To find out how to meditate read on. The changes will occur all right and you don't have to do a thing – except do the practice… and find the time.

Thanks, Henry...

I owe a debt of deep gratitude to Henry Rennox who agreed to pose for the photographs in this book while he was at HMP Springhill. This is Henry's story:

"I was born in Scotland, had a terrible childhood, and then I went to Canada from where I was later deported. This is my fourteenth sentence. For years, I was a violent, angry, hateful person, very bigoted and prejudiced. I was abused as a child and one day when I was sitting in meditation, in my mind I saw my father, his father and my own son and I realised how easy it could be to repeat what my father had done to me to my own son. I had tried all drugs (and not all came from a local dealer either). Once I stayed awake for 14 days on drugs just to see what it was like. The start of this sentence at HMP Lewes saw me having lost my family, my children, my home, my business.

"I was in a lot of pain and someone told me there was a yoga class where they did relaxation. When I told the person who became my teacher that I was a drug addict, she suggested I should stop punishing myself. Twelve months later I realised she was right. I used to try to learn everything that came my way all at once and then I'd get fed up with it. I used to pick up things to please other people. Now, I am doing something for myself at last.

"I moved from Lewes to Maidstone prison next, where there were stabbings, burnings, beatings and drugs during my time there. It was a great temptation to slip back. There was no place to practise yoga, apart from my cell, and no class. So I emptied out my cell, apart from the bed, and kept it just for my yoga. Then the others started to notice and the lads did too. A couple got interested and I started to teach them what I knew. It made me feel better.

"After a year I moved to Springhill and the yoga teacher here helped me a lot. Many people have helped since I started on the path. It seems to me that whenever I have really needed something — or someone — it comes along. Everything really, spiritual help, whatever, someone has always been there.

"The first thing I came to understand is that people have to want to change. They think when the sentence comes to an end, the pain is all over. Meditation helped me understand that that isn't so, perhaps because I was in enough pain to see it. I meditate every morning and evening. If I had to say to someone what yoga has done for me I guess it is to say it has made me happy ..."

Becoming Free through Meditation

By Sister Elaine MacInnes

Sister Elaine with ex-political prisoners.

Meditation and the art of doing time

I first set foot inside a prison when I was in the Philippines during the worst of the Marcos years. Like all oppressive regimes, it was supported by a powerful Intelligence Service. All kinds of fear and violence surfaced and the brunt was borne by the poor. As it happened, the community to which I belong — Our Lady's Missionaries — serve the poor there in the countryside. In fact, one of our sisters had, at one time, to stand her trial in Manila for aiding subversives.

The early eighties were such bad years that the Meditation Centre was under continual threat of abduction and so I was given shelter by the Good Shepherd sisters who also work with the poor, in their convent.

One hot summer's evening, a whispered phone message came that Boy Morales (a well-known dissident who had been dreadfully tortured for ten days) wanted me to teach him Zen meditation in prison. As the phone was tapped, the request couldn't be discussed then but a meeting was arranged later. After several secret meetings and after approaching the Canadian Ambassador for help, he was able to arrange my safety in setting up a meditation day, once a week, at Bago Bantay Detention Centre. In no time at all, Morales got almost the entire group of detainees — 12 in all — to sit together, a practice which served them well during their five year-long incarceration in the appalling conditions of that Philipinno prison.

A woman dreamed she walked into a brand-new shop in the marketplace and, to her surprise, found God behind the counter.
'What do you sell here?' she asked.
'Everything your heart desires,' said God.
Hardly daring to believe what she was hearing, the woman decided to ask for the best things a human being could wish for.
'I want peace of mind and love and happiness and wisdom and freedom from fear,' she said.
Then as an afterthought she added, 'Not just for me, for everyone on earth.'
God smiled, 'I think you've got me wrong, my dear,' He said. 'We don't sell fruits here. Only seeds.'

Seeking to ease the pain

I never feel we at the Prison Phoenix have to sell meditation. Today there just seems to be an invisible magnet reaching all over the world, attracting certain people, who for some reason or other, are aware of what can be experienced in meditation and want to try it. I know that not all of us who live at the same time experience the same things, so there will be many who do not feel this way. We respect them, whilst still addressing the growing number who seek to ease the pain and darkness of our lonely era, by means of meditation. I find it not at all surprising that many such people are in our prison population.

When scientists designate our time as the age of 'chaos', it is to be expected that some of us experience its uncertainty and fragility. Many of the old props and sureties have disappeared! And in a religious sense, what has been taken away is encountered in the ache of its loss.

I am always struck by the fact that the home of a prisoner and a monk are indicated by the same word 'cell'. We at the Trust often say in our writings that a prisoner's cell is not unlike the retreat rooms we go to every once in a while for silence and reflection. They are inclined to be small, with only a bed, table and chair. And we go to the cell to deal with pain and darkness, for the human spirit is always trying to transcend itself, spontaneously searching for life and light.

A recent letter from a prisoner brought all this in focus: *"As long as I can remember, I have had this hurt inside. I can't get away from it, and sometimes I cut or burn myself so that the pain will be in a different place and on the outside. Then I saw your newsletter last month, and something spoke to me about meditation and although I didn't really know what it is, I wrote for your book. I just want you to know that after only four weeks of meditating, a half hour in the morning and at night, for the first time in my life, I see a tiny spark of something within myself that I can like."*

Sister Elaine

The sleeping child

To concretize the reality of WHO WE ARE, is at best a risky venture. Help came unexpectedly recently, when we received a letter from an inmate containing the following paragraph :

> *"I know that the spiritual child is sleeping inside us all.*
> *All beings, no matter how reactionary, fearful, dangerous or lost,*
> *can open up and be free. I am free even in prison."*

And during a visit to HMP Wandsworth, one of our meditation teachers was using the child image, which she had read about in a book by the popular Vietnamese Buddhist monk, Thich Nhat Hahn. He was discussing the problems one has in the midst of any high feelings especially around fear, and advised us all to calm those feelings by being one with them, just like a mother tenderly holding her crying child. Feeling his mother's tenderness, the baby will stop crying and gradually calm down.

However, do not look at that child as a separate entity. That child is YOU.

"Heavens how you've aged!"
exclaimed the Master after
speaking with a childhood friend.
"One cannot help growing old,
can one?" said the friend.
"No, one cannot," agreed the
Master, "but one must avoid
becoming aged."

A woman in distress over
the death of her son came to
the Master for comfort.
He listened to her patiently
while she poured out her
tale of woe.
Then he said softly, "I
cannot wipe away your tears, my
dear. I can only teach
you that they are holy."

To a preacher
who kept saying,
"We must put God
into our lives,"
the Master said
"God is already there.
Our business
is to recognize this."

Dear Sister,

Life is so short.

I just had my 30th birthday and I keep thinking I'm not 30 yet, still 16 or 18. I just don't feel grown up, but then I think, what does grown up feel like? Or 'old' feel like?

When Bo said 'what would make you happy' I said 'out of here', he said 'there's plenty of people out there who are unhappy'. Fair enough, there are. But the way I mean it was I've got plans, when I get out, and I see in here as a block in my path - but I may have to rearrange my plan if I'm found guilty.

I made up a prayer which I say every night. I settle in my bed 'cause I'm in a ward. The TV is usually on till 1 a.m. but that does not interfere with my routine. I do a few stretches and watch a few breaths to relax myself, then I begin:

Respected fathers, far and away, thank you for guiding me today.
Respected fathers, high and above, shower down on me your love.
Respected fathers, what you can do, grant me wisdom and courage to see me through.
Respected fathers, you must look down through the clouds and shed a tear at what you see, the sadness, the lost souls, I also shed a tear at what I see, maybe we are one.
Respected fathers grant me serenity, wisdom, courage and faith, and let tomorrow look after tomorrow.

I don't know why, Sister, but I really feel like that and I believe someone's looking after me even though I'm in this mess.

From HMP Brixton

Our own healing breath

Generally speaking, in the Orient, meditation teaches people how to use their own healing breath. The early writings of both the East and West speak of the sacredness of the breath. The main spiritual practice of almost all the Oriental religions is based on the breath, but how this came to be, is lost in history. The Christian Bible says that we became living beings by God breathing into us. Not only is the breath sacred, but when we deal with it, we are dealing with the Life Force—the vivifying force—within us. This is the most powerful force in the universe, and also the source of all power that exists.

Great care has to be taken that its use is geared towards health and healing. There are misuses that can incite even a healthy psyche, not to mention if you are one of those writing to us about getting your head straight. Psychologists and psychiatrists can help you do that. The teachers in the Trust believe that a most effective way of 'getting your head right' also is to let the Power within the breath do its own thing, which is to work on the blocks that prevent our head working the way it should.

Our meditation is very simple, almost deceptively so. Many of the disciplines coming out of the Orient have a lot of pre-suppositions, but not our Way. It IS simple, because once you have the body in place, you really don't have to do anything but be one with your breath, because this procedure cuts out thoughts. Our rule-of-thumb is to silence the body by the appropriate posture, and silence the mind through breath awareness. Then silence itself will do its work. It may sound strange to new ears, but not only is it possible, it can also be said to be inevitable.

If your meditation is based on silence, you will not only automatically experience the therapeutic effects which sitting (meditation is often referred to as 'sitting') brings, and which I will discuss later, but also brings into play the real operator in our discipline, which is the Sacred. To become a disciple of this Power is the root of the word, discipline.

Perhaps here is a good spot to remind our readers that the Prison Phoenix Trust works with people of any religion, or of none. I know of no religion which does not recognize a Power greater than itself, although IT may have different tags or names. As a Christian, I call that power God. The Buddhists with whom I studied in Japan referred to IT as the Buddha Nature. God and Buddha Nature are tags for the Sacred which vivifies all of creation.

Steady as she goes

"All the 45 years of my life, I have been searching for something and have never felt fulfilled. Probably why I've had so many relationships. I have a very active mind - can't relax - so I read four or five books at a time, as much TV and radio and newspapers as I can, just anything. Because when it goes quiet or I'm not concentrating or something, I feel very frightened and all my emotions boil over. I cry a lot and feel unstable. Being in a cell on my own is not helping, cause I'm sinking into my natural and reserved and depressed state. When I do get the chance to talk with Samaritans, counsellors, probation officers etc. here, I can't stop talking. It all comes gushing out, my emotions and stress and anxiety. I go from one extreme to another not saying anything hour after hour, and then pouring everything out when I get the chance. When am I going to get my head right! I am trying meditation, and yes I'm finding it hard but I intend to persevere because whatever happens to me, I must find some strength within."

You don't have to try to do the impossible by blotting out your unhappiness. But you can use it to help you come to terms with the past. Along the way, you'll discover all kinds of surprising things including some things about yourself which you CAN love. Meditation isn't easy, but it is a good deal easier than the extremely difficult road you are travelling at the moment. The Oriental masters believe that it is an over-active ego which leads to offending behaviour (yours and mine) because it becomes the chief operating agent and acts only for itself. How refreshing to be free of this inner pressure. For thousands of years, they have recognized that we all have an inner power which is greater than ourselves. By allowing it to heal body and mind, simply by sitting in silence, we can change our lives. But we have to do that for ourselves!

What is needed for meditation

Loose baggy clothing is a must for sitting – like your tracksuit trousers. Nothing is more detrimental to a good sitting posture than tight jeans - sorry about that - but try it once and you'll see what I mean.

The tools for sitting are a folded blanket or large squarish soft pad, so that your feet and ankles rest comfortably on it. If you are meditating on a mattress, then that is sufficient. On top of that is needed a small cushion — preferably round, and about 4 inches high to support the spine.

It is universally called a 'zafu' and perhaps you can make one for yourself.

Directions For Making a Zafu

1. Using a length of cloth approximately 95 inches long and six inches wide, pin in two-inch pleats, two inches apart

2. Pin in two circles of cloth, each with a diameter of 10 inches, to pleated strip, one at the top, one at the bottom.

3. Ease the pleats into the circle and stitch.

4. Turn inside out and stuff to desired height with a mixture of foam chips and kapok.

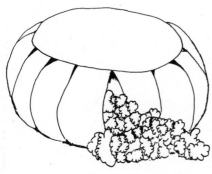

The Instant Meditation Bench:
You need a plank about 2cm thick,
15cm wide, 82cm long....

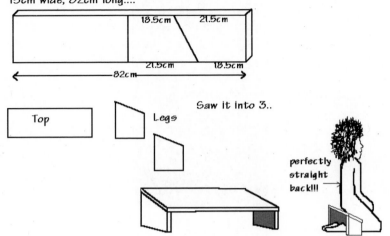

Saw it into 3..

Top

Legs

perfectly
straight
back!!!

you can put it together with metal 90° brackets
OR wooden pegs and glue
    OR with screws

it isn't strong enough if you just use nails

The measurements can be wider or higher to suit your body and legs.

If you aren't able to make or find a zafu or meditation bench, it is a good idea to improvise with whatever you have in your cell. You could use:

* Folded pillows

* A few books

* A jumper and jacket

* An upturned washing up bowl

All that matters is that you are comfortable and have at least four inches under your bottom. Don't forget that you can also sit upright in a chair or on the edge of your bed, with your feet flat on the floor.

Full Lotus

Half Lotus

Burmese

Seiza

Using Bench

Using Chair

Silencing the body

The appropriate positioning of the body is based upon the teachings of yogis. What's important is a sitting posture that keeps the back, neck, and head in a straight line, in such a way that there is no tension required to hold the body in place. I shall give more detailed instructions.

Put the zafu at the centre back of the folded blanket, and sit on the front half of it, with your legs extended out in front. Bend the left knee and tuck the left foot above the right thigh. Bend your right knee, and taking the right foot in hand, push the right knee to the floor, and place the right foot on the thigh of the left leg. Yogis tell us that all activity starts on the right side of the body, so if we are in the process of silencing the body, we 'pin down' the right side first. If we can do the same with the left side, then we have achieved the most difficult but also the best position of the legs and feet. It is called the full lotus. For beginners, an easier position is the half-lotus:

1. Straighten out the legs in front,
2. Bend the right knee, tuck the right foot in close to the body,
3. Take the left foot in your right hand,
4. Push the left knee to the floor,
5. Place the left foot on the right thigh,
6. Adjust the positioning of the spine on the zafu.

This is the most common position. It can be reversed by tucking the left foot in towards the body and putting the right foot on the left thigh. The half lotus is not as symmetrical as the full lotus, but is more available to most of us. Keep the knees down. When they are touching the mat, the back is almost naturally straight.

The other possible leg positions are :

Burmese   Both legs lying bent and parallel on the mat.

Kneeler   Tuck a rectangular bench under the thighs and buttocks.

Seiza   Tuck in a couple of zafus from a kneeling position.

Chair   If all else fails, use a flat stool (no leaning). A low one with a zafu is the best.

Sit the way you can. For steadiness, form a tripod, with the two knees and buttocks. If one or both knees cannot reach the floor, fill in the space with a small auxiliary cushion or pad. Keep the spine straight, using decreasing arc movements until it falls naturally into position. After the legs are in place, lean forward once, extending the flesh of the buttocks backwards, and then straighten up. Muscles must not be used to hold up the backbone, and its curve is maintained.

A former inmate of a Nazi concentration camp was visiting someone who had shared the ordeal with him.

'Have you forgiven the Nazis?' he asked his friend.

'Yes'

'Well I haven't. I'm still consumed with hatred for them.'

'In that case,' said his friend gently, 'they still have you in prison.'

Silencing the mind

Meditation can be a great help in releasing our minds from the tyranny of relentless thoughts. If you long to find a more peaceful way of being, meditation is a wonderful tool but like everything new, it takes time and daily practice. A longing for peace is the perfect motivation for meditating. It will help sustain you during your practice and, if you are determined, your longing will be answered.

First of all, don't worry about thoughts popping up. The brain is programmed to think. It's what it does. On the other hand, when you switch your attention from your thoughts to your breath and allow your breath to absorb all your being and focus, in time the busy mind quietens down. It doesn't happen all at once.

On some days you may need all your courage to stay still, breathing through whatever comes up interrupting your breath attention. But gradually you'll see for yourself that when you sit you never sit alone. We sit within a universal compassion too vast for anyone of us to comprehend with the thinking mind. But our unknowing minds know its compassionate solace and help just when we need it.

By the way, when your mind is diverted by thoughts don't worry. Just accept what is happening as a "necessary washing". It's part of the process of meditation and as soon as you notice you have lost your breath attention, bring it back onto the breath again.

Your daily practice is always alive because it is constantly changing just as the silence at the depths of your being always embracing you. Some days meditation may seem simple but hard, and on other times, something you look forward to and enjoy. If you find yourself able to maintain a regular practice the real you will slowly emerge and you'll find it is a person you can appreciate very much.

Taking off

"All you need for meditation is your body, your mind, and your breath. Being shut in your cell for much of the day provides you with an excellent opportunity for practice, and for change."

Ann Wetherall, founder of the PPT

Said a world-famous violinist about his success in playing a piece by Beethoven, 'I have splendid music, a splendid violin, and a splendid bow. All I need to do is bring them together and get out of the way'.

And above all let go of your tension …

Just let it drop off

The following body position helps us to allow this to happen.

The positioning of the hands is called mudra, a Sanskrit term meaning 'seal'. Rest the wrists on the thighs, and keeping the hands open, put the left hand in the right, with the middle knuckles touching and the tips of the thumbs meeting and pulled towards the body to form an oval. As I said above, this positioning of the hands connects energy cycles which, according to ancient Chinese medicine, course through the meridians of the body.

We all know that our spine, seen from the side, is not straight. It is almost an elongated 'S'. A short and safe rule of thumb is just to sit tall, and make sure that the curve in the small of the back is maintained. If there is a teacher going regularly to your prison, s/he will frequently just touch that spot to indicate you are slouching. When corrected, your sitting posture will be about two or three centimetres higher.

Incidentally, many of the teachers in the Orient say that if you want distractions, just slouch. If you want to cut down on distractions, then sit tall, almost as though you want to touch the ceiling with the top of your head. Keep the chin tucked in slightly.

Seen from the front or back, the spine can be naturally straight. I have found many people to have a curvature of the spine called scoliosis. In many cases, it is congenital, and not much can be done about it. Just try to keep your head in a straight line with the backbone.

However, it is also a general habit for us to lean slightly to the left or right or forward or backward, as we concentrate in one-pointedness. If you are lucky enough to have teachers monitoring, then they will pull you into position. If there is no teacher, then try to check your own position occasionally.

All our senses should remain open, so keep the eyes merely resting on a spot about one metre in front of the nose. If you are meditating well, your eyes will probably go out of focus on occasion.

Keep the mouth closed, the teeth not clenched, and with the tongue resting on the front upper teeth. This will control the flow of saliva.

Sitting's not easy !

Sitting is not complicated - although not easy, it is very simple. In a kind of general way, you have first to allow yourself to be emptied. Secondly, let go, so there will be no fear of emptiness. Thirdly, stop day-dreaming.

At Wandsworth Prison, some of the men in the meditation class said they don't have any trouble whilst sitting together, but it all comes apart when they return to the wing.

That doesn't have to happen. Peace of mind is an inner happening and if we just try to stay with one thing at a time, all the other pulls become weaker. The pressure can then come off. Unfortunately at the moment there is not much hope of sitting together daily in meditation. Maybe one day!

Breathing

There are many theories of breathing to be found in spiritual books, but the simple rule we advocate is to breathe naturally. The fact that we start with breath concentration means that we will pay more attention to the way we breathe, and consequently there may be a slight deepening and/or slowing of the inhalations and exhalations. However, we never TRY to breathe differently. Exceptionally deep breathing over an extended period of time can make us dizzy and we start to wobble. Physical stability is very important in meditating.

Feel and know each breath as if it is the first breath you have ever taken.

Once the body is in position, start to concentrate in one-pointedness, by counting the breaths. Count '1' on the first inhalation, and '2' on its exhalation ; then '3' on the next inhalation, and '4' on its exhalation. Repeat this sequence until 10, and then go back to 1. It is said that we can count to 10 in our own language without activating the mind too much.

There is an eight week sitting programme on the next page. Try to stick to this programme for a couple of months, and see if you have developed the technique for becoming absorbed in your breathing, which will be there when you need it.

The correct way to breathe is through the nose, with the lips kept lightly resting together. The air coming into the body needs to be filtered, and the nose contains a most efficient system designed for just that. Also, the air needs to be warmed by the mucous membrane in the nostrils or the respiratory organs can become inflamed, and the air needs to be moistened which takes place in the nose as well.

And try to savour occasionally, the healing fact that the breath is the seat of the Life of the Sacred within.

An eight week programme of meditation

If you are a beginner, then select your best sitting position as found on page 70. Start each sit with the following sequence: Take a very slow and deep inhalation, hold it for a couple of seconds, and then exhale all of it. Rest. Then take another slow and deep inhalation and exhalation, and rest, and then finally repeat this once more. Now you are ready to start.

How to do breath counting

Breathing naturally, and watching the breath, count each inhalation and each exhalation up to 10. The first inhalation is 1, the first exhalation is 2, the second inhalation is 3, and the second exhalation is 4 etc. Once you have reached 10, return to 1.

Eventually, try to eliminate the duality of you and the breath, by BEING ONE WITH YOUR BREATH.

It is not something that you can acquire by just wanting it. It just comes on its own, hesitantly at first, and then gradually with more regularity and assurance. It comes by practice.

Week 1 and 2

Count each inhalation and each exhalation as directed above.

Week 3 and 4

Just count the inhalations, and watch the exhalations.

Week 5 and 6

Watch the inhalations, and count the exhalations, still up to 10. This way is the most natural.

Weeks 7 and 8

Try to be one with each inhalation and exhalation, not using any counting. This is difficult, but give it a try.

Now when you have finished the eight week programme, and feel the effect of your sitting, then you may want to continue. I suggest you take the practise of the way you counted the breaths during weeks 5 and 6, watching the inhalations, and counting the exhalations. Eventually, for short periods, you may be able to hold on one-pointedly without counting. This is very peace-giving, but usually cannot be sustained very long. When your mind begins to wander and distractions appear, then calmly put them aside, and return to the counting. Everybody has some distractions, so don't get discouraged. Silent meditation is very subtle and the dividends you receive will be well worth the effort. After a while, if something comes up and prevents your meditation, you will miss your sitting.

Remember now you have the time!

Use it !

A man who took great pride in his lawn found himself with a large crop of dandelions. He tried every method he knew to get rid of them. Still they plagued him.

Finally he wrote to the Department of Agriculture. He enumerated all the things he had tried and closed his letter with the question:

'What shall I do now?'

In due course the reply came:

'We suggest you learn to love them.'

Duration of time for sitting

For a beginner, the duration of meditation is a very personal matter. It first of all depends on the length of time in which you can maintain the body position without moving. Beginners are urged to get down on the floor and try one of the sitting positions, for the body can help the mind. But unless the body is particularly supple, most of the positions will not be possible for some time. Perhaps you could kneel and then sit on a bench or two cushions. That is easy enough for anyone without knee joint problems. So start there, if that is what you can do easily at first, and stick with it until you can manage the more involved positions. If you wish to become a serious meditation student then practise some of the yoga suggestions at the front of this book so that you become more supple. In time you will not only sit well in the half-lotus position, but it will gradually become indispensable for you.

The very best measure is to time yourself and see how long you can hold the position you are in, without moving. If you can sit for ten minutes quite still and without pain, then sit for ten minutes, and follow that with a five minute walking meditation.

Walking meditation is called kinhin, during which time you walk slowly, whilst continuing breath-counting. Fist the right hand, and cover it with the left palm and fingers. The eyes rest on the floor about one metre in front. Then walk slowly allowing the leg muscles and tendons to flex gently and return the blood-flow to normal. This takes about five minutes. Even if the walking room in your cell is miniscule, a determined meditator will make it do.

The rhythm we use at all our meditation centres is: 25 minute sitting, and five minute kinhin. If possible, we do this three times. Of course this is a bit extreme for most beginners, so we suggest that you start the way you can, not only with the sitting posture, but also in the time duration. If you can do only the Burmese position for twelve minutes, then just do that. That's fine. However, aim for the half-lotus position, and try to maintain it for 25 minutes.

The ideal sitting time is in the early morning when we arise and the mind is free from distractions of interesting and vivid linear thoughts and pictures. Do two sits then, and possibly two sits in the evening before retiring. Such a practice would be an ideal discipline, and will reveal results quite soon.

Dear Sister,

Thanks for your letter. I've just had some good–bad news depending which way I look at it. My date of the 6th December has been adjourned to the 7th of March. It's quite a long way off but I'm not really angry as I was kind of expecting for the date to be so long away. So three months to wait. So by the time I go up it will be nearly ten months I've been in.

I'm in a tricky situation Sr Elaine. I've been offered to plead guilty to manslaughter and probably get five years or go through with the trial for murder. My counsel and Barrister reckon the outcome could be :

25% found guilty of murder = life (mandatory)

50% found guilty of manslaughter = seven or eight years

25% found not guilty = walk free

or, plead guilty to manslaughter and get in the region of five years. My counsel told me it's a gamble and I hold the dice. Sister I DON'T KNOW WHAT TO DO, I FEEL CRUSHED. Honest I'm at a dead end on this one, I need help from somewhere. It's making me feel up tight very much so could you please help me in some way Sister?

Love,

From Brixton prison

So much in life SEEMS to have no answer.

Difficulties you may encounter in meditating

Fear

Lowering of the eyes in a prison situation is unfamiliar, so you may experience fear at first. Of course in some circumstances there is cause for fear. But, we can create a trusting environment for ourselves and the short time we spend meditating daily, will be safe for us, leaving behind even our wary circumspection.

Dizziness

This is usually caused by incorrect breathing, so spend time getting a solid body position (one old master used to say, 'sit like a mountain' which is still good advice), then breathe naturally, not too deep, not too slow, nor unsteadily.

A buzz

A buzz is an altered state of consciousness, and is not to be cultivated. Any such state requires an accompanying technique in order to bring about a healing effect. States like trance or hypnosis must be supported by experts and not indulged in for a 'kick', or the result can be disastrous. During meditation, when anything other than breath awareness enters the consciousness, it can be expelled by returning to the practice, for the consciousness cannot operate integrally with a 'double' presence.

Drugs also bring about an altered state of consciousness. Historically, we know they were often used for spiritual or medicinal purposes, and always in a controlled and monitored situation. We are sometimes asked by drug users in prison, if we recommend drugs as a help for meditation, and the answer is an unequivocal 'no'. It cuts down the power of concentration.

Can meditation help to kick the habit?

That obviously depends. It would seem best in most cases to ask for help. Many prisons have a hospital wing in which they treat drug addiction, followed by a drug free wing for rehabilitation. I would think a meditation programme supporting such regimes would have a good chance for success.

Inner noise

It could be that some of you will feel that breath-counting becomes too noisy eventually ... that there is too much going on. Then, you 'just sit' in one-pointedness. If you have really developed this far, then you will understand what it means, and be able to do it and remain absorbed in your sitting. Congratulations. You are well on the way to finding out who you are.

83

Therapeutic effects of mature sitting

I always have some reservations about discussing the effects of meditation, because it seems to be out of balance in the West today. Of course it's true, that people meditate to slow down their heartbeat, or give them a measure of stress management. But for the meditation masters of old, these are merely side issues, or 'perks'.

On the other hand, they are real helps in prison pressures today, and especially perhaps in the healing of old wounds and blocks, deep in the psyche. So let us take a short look at them, as presented by the masters of old.

If we meditate regularly and well :

1. Our dissipated energies gradually become more unified.

2. We start to gain some control over our superactive mind.

3. Tensions are released.

4. Nerves become relaxed.

5. Our physical health generally improves.

6. Emotions are sensitized.

7. The will strengthened.

8. We begin to experience a kind of inner balance.

9. Gradually dryness, rigidity, hangups, prejudices, and egotism, melt.

10. And then compassion, serenity, egolessness, and social concern can freely surface.

Of course all this does not happen in a day. But the fact that it does happen, and that influences of it are felt quite soon after starting to meditate, gives us hope and courage to continue. By the same token, it has to be admitted, that this silent meditation is neither interesting nor entertaining. It is also interesting and entertaining …

REMEMBER WE ARE NOT MEDITATING TO BE ENTERTAINED

WE ARE DOING MEDITATION IN ORDER TO CHANGE

AND EVENTUALLY TO FIND OUT WHO WE ARE !

No ego!

A woodcarver called Ching had just finished work on a bell frame. Everyone who saw it marvelled, for it seemed to be the work of spirits. When the Duke of Lu saw it, he asked, 'What sort of genius is yours that you could make such a thing ?'

The woodcarver replied, 'Sire, I am only a simple workman, I am no genius. But there is one thing. When I am going to make a bell frame, I meditate for three days to calm my mind. When I have meditated for three days, I think no more about rewards or emoluments. When I have meditated for five days, I no longer think of praise or blame, skilfullness or awkwardness. When I have meditated for seven days, I suddenly forget my limbs, my body; no, I forget my very self. I lose consciousness of the course and my surroundings. Only my skill remains.

'In that state I walk into the forest and examine each tree until I find one in which I see the bell frame in all its perfection. Then my hands go to the task. Having set my self aside, nature meets nature in the work that is performed through me. This, no doubt, is the reason why everyone says that the finished product is the work of spirits.'

Awakening to WHO you are

I have before me a letter from H.M.Prison Canterbury in Kent, which says: *"The real reason I am writing to you is because I can feel my life changing. I know I'm a long way off of KNOWING ME. If I knew I wouldn't be writing to you now, but there is still some confusion going on in my head and I want some help."*

The first thing we usually notice after we have started to practice regularly, is that we feel refreshed after sitting. Later, that seems to deepen into a kind of attitude change, which brightens up the world for us. We start to feel really good about ourselves and our life. Then we get happier as we notice change in the way we perceive people and things and happenings, that they are all part of something special and Sacred.

And finally we come to that flash of intuition, when we reach, in our practice, a way of KNOWING. We are awakened to WHO we really are. This is a moment of great joy. And no matter what your past was, what you have done or what you haven't done ... you are ecstatic and humbled about WHO you really are.

In the East this is called the time when you 'see your own Nature'. Many people come to a Meditation Centre simply because they want to experience this. That may involve a special method of teaching, but only in the sense that it brings one along more quickly to that experience. Everyone who sits in silent meditation is on that Path, and will sooner or later come to the experience, if they persevere.

For the beginner, the experience is partly described in the letter quoted on page 63: the inmate who said after meditating for only two weeks, he saw a tiny spark of something within himself that he could actually like. That is the sort of happening that may be only barely noticeable at first, but with more sitting, the 'real you' takes on a deeper meaning, and holds out great hope and possibility.

In our branch of meditation, we usually invite the sitter to write about their experience, and here follows partial accounts by three prisoners (in Manila, Philippines, from 1984 to 86).

Letters from prisoners

The first account of the experience is in the form of a letter from Marcello, who had been arrested five times, tortured each time, blindfolded, and harassed almost beyond human endurance. He entitled his letter to me,

Bars of no-iron

My dear Sister Elaine,

It has been a year and two months since you confirmed my awakening experience, yet it is only now that I write to you about it. Please forgive me.

I have tried many times to put that experience on paper but I could never seem to finish it. This is one of the very few times in my life I have tried to write in English. But I found that even if I tried to say it in Filipino, the words still would not come! In no language can I write what I want to say! Can I just say that I have NOTHING AND EVERYTHING to write about, because I now know how to say something without moving my lips or tongue!

You confirmed my experience last year on my birthday, which is the Feast of the Virgin Mary's birthday too! It was on that day and during that celebration I joyously announced, "I am perfectly free, I am perfectly happy, and deeply at peace!" This was possible, because even though in prison, I had tasted of the true ONENESS you led me to in meditation.

I did not tell you this before, but for some time previous to the experience, I thought I had already tasted 'it'. I was very aware that something was happening to me, and I was very happy, even though incarcerated. You just kept bringing me along in my sitting, until the REAL IT happened, at a very unforgettable moment. For me, that moment defies all description. I was so overwhelmed that my wife and companions could not help but notice the change in my face and manners.

That night, back in my cell, I slept soundly like a baby, with a smile on my lips. Now I know that where I am and where I want to be, are no different at all! The bars and stone walls do not really separate me from my loved ones, from my friends, from my people, and from everything and everybody in the universe. In reality, I and the universe are one.

Thank you!

*'Know thyself' calls attention
to the depth dimension of one's
being.*

*It helps discover one's
roots in the eternal.*

Silent meditation leads to a revelation of the Self. When we come to know this True Self, we will discover who we are.

One of the great sages of our time, Abishiktananda, says that to experience this is the highest possible attainment for the human being.

There are of course degrees into the depth of this experience, as well as individualities. There are also common points. A teacher will often invite the sitter to write something about the experience.

In the spiritual sense, toleration is an act of love and understanding.

Love opens the door to the appreciation of opposite viewpoints.

The blade of grass

The second partial account is by a young woman prisoner, Rosanna, who apparently during meditation decided to close her eyes for a moment in savouring. By way of interest, I'd like to say that this happened just before the revolution, and there were only two prisoners sitting with me at the time. As usual, I had gone early that day to clean the room, and found there was an old piece of withered grass growing amongst the broken cement, coming up through the floor. I tried unsuccessfully to pull it out. The two sitters entered and we started meditation. Rosanna, who had been in prison for four years, caught a glimpse of 'who she is' during that meditation, and she wrote a poem about it:

February 15 did not seem to be of any
special significance to me
although the day before, I kept asking
questions about love and its importance.
I asked what ways are there to show love
and why we Filipinos seem to be sentimental
about celebrating it on February 14.
Why not on every one of the 365 days of
the year, every year ?
I never expected the insights that came
to me that day,
sitting with Sister Elaine and Boy in the
visiting room at the usual schedule,
Friday, from 10 to 2 in the afternoon.
I sat with an empty mind and an open self
closing my eyes and savouring every bit
of my calmness and emptiness
until the time came that I felt like
opening my eyes.
I SAW THE DRIEST BLADE OF GRASS
SPROUTING THROUGH THE CONCRETE FLOOR
SEEING IT WAS SEEING MYSELF
HEARING THE ANSWERS TO ALL MY QUESTIONS,
UNDERSTANDING WITH ALL MY SOUL.
In the coldest concrete floor
there is warmth, there is love.
In the driest blade of grass
Life flows, love grows.

Through a prison window

The third and final partial account is from a young man 'Boy' who had been awarded the highest medal of distinction in the country, and who nevertheless went on to join the peoples' struggle against the Marcos regime. He was especially pursued and caught and tortured in the early 80s. He entitled the articulation of his experience 'Through a Prison Window'. A selection of its contents runs as follows :

My arrest and detention confronted me with a totally different situation. Although my colleagues and I tried to prepare for all contingencies, detention affected me in very specific ways that I could not have foreseen. While under detention, events would happen outside prison that had adverse effects on me personally, and I found it frustrating that there was almost nothing I could do in response.

But being confined is also an opportunity to take stock of things, to reflect and refresh oneself. I was very glad therefore to learn about the Zendo and the work being done by Sister Elaine. I had always been interested in Zen, and so decided with some of my co-detainees to invite Sister Elaine for orientation talks on how to sit and meditate.

(It soon became clear to me that) the three sets of changes that had transpired in my life, having to do with people, things and events, and my perception of these changes, all seemed to suggest that the key to my search for self fulfilment lay in the resolution of the constant tension between me and the rest of existence. All of this came to naught one wonderful moment in the middle of an April night.

After our orientation sessions, and despite our restricted circumstances, we practised sitting regularly, and Sister Elaine gave us weekly teisho (Zen talks) and dokusan (Zen interviews). Seven out of the nine detainees participated in the orientation and sitting, and we made it a point to sit together every day at noon. Visitors are not allowed between 12 and 2, and also the lunch break is the only time we are noisefree from the adjacent firing range and motor pool!

We are locked in our individual cells daily from 8 p.m. until 8 a.m. I sit every night and find these periods very conducive to deep sitting, even though it is almost impossible to do kinhin (walking meditation) since the length of the cell is only 3 steps and there is no width! But one night I sat for a couple of hours, and then as I was doing one such kinhin, all the tensions and the inner struggles suddenly dissolved into nothing, and a new boundless Union only, existed! At that particular moment, instantaneous yet Infinite, I was awakened to the Essential World!

How true the assertion that the experience is incommunicable! Now that I look back on it, I can say with certainty that I 'saw' Emptiness and then ONENESS, and intimacy and harmony and appropriateness which made me 'see' the happiness and beauty in everything, but at that moment the whole universe was in my prison cell, and Sister Elaine who was sick in Canada was not separate either. When she returned some months later and confirmed this experience as authentic, I was almost not surprised. I have absolute faith in what happened to me. I know I can abandon myself to ITS Way, and rest assured in this new perspective.

Now it seems to me that I see all things more clearly. Not only are the answers evident, the questions are irrelevant. To question changing roles in life may not even be the way to seek our true Self Nature. Once we know our True Self, the different roles we assume no longer bother us. Getting rid of garbage in sitting, our True Self will gradually be able to do the appropriate thing, and fit into any role that may be required. Thus we never get lost and always are fulfilled.

Let's not be distracted by questions of roles, self-image, or even reputation. Although these are important, we cannot come to know our True Nature by starting with them. Underlying such concerns is a delusion which strengthens the ego. In the same way, getting overly concerned about the higher meaning of life suggests a presumption that one has a more 'special' existence than others.

Since that night I don't feel the need to be more assertive, or more self-effacing, or more defensive. I am trying to give free-expression to my true Self Nature, and gradually become spontaneous and egoless and nonthreatening. When we can so act at each juncture of time, we will act as self-fulfilled beings.

Zen says there's already a flow in action. Let us allow ourselves to go with it and to respond appropriately to the imperatives of our times. What are our real needs and the needs of our people now? What are the things that are holding us back from responding to these imperatives? Since we had no choice about the time of our birth, our presence at this point in time when there are tremendous changes and movements in our society, gives us a unique challenge and opportunity to be more concerned and active socially. Perhaps we will be taken to other things besides these concerns. Wherever it goes, we will be carried to the same place!

I don't get obstructed by prison walls any more, nor am I anxious about how our case will be eventually settled. Through my prison window, I can see IT pervades the whole universe, and I am in my perfect place, moving along the Way.

Right now the prison walls are down, and I am roaming and romping about! At the crack of dawn, the surroundings are resplendent, and the fields are verdant. In a short while, we will wake up to a new spring when everything will be new.

"The joy of the raindrop is in entering the ocean."

A Zen quotation

Getting to know how it feels

Going to prison once a week meant understanding at first hand how it feels to have no assurance of welcome from prison officers who kept up a hostile battle for four and a half years. I got used to guards with their guns up and threatening but I was often frightened. And for one day each week, it was good to know how it feels sharing those conditions with them and the rest of the prison community.

The worse thing was that during all that time, anyone who helped me with transport was put at risk. License plates were often noted by the Intelligence with bad consequences. In the end, a ten-minutes stay in a nearby church acted as a decoy, especially since it had many doors to exit by, so the prison could be reached by a variety of routes.

And each time the twelve detainees were waiting, in the dirty little cement three-sided room, which had no windows in those tropical temperatures. After we had swept out the dirt and set up the altar, the group set down the cushions they had brought and we began. In spite of the hostile atmosphere we had great sittings in meditation and were able to share a meal together afterwards – a ceremony which is very important in the Orient.

Why am I including this account of those years here? I think it is because those people had been so badly tortured, and sometimes their whole bodies seemed to shake. The prison was derelict and although I've seen many prisons in the UK which badly need improvement, nothing could touch Bago Bantay for bleakness. Yet in spite of all that, this group of prisoners benefited tremendously from their meditation experience which they continued faithfully during the week when they were on their own. When Boy Morales ran for the Senate years later, he was able to say that the peak experience of his life had been during his prison sentence when he was meditating. It encouraged me greatly to hear that and I hope it encourages you too, dear friends.

'Over the past year and a half, I've accomplished more inside prison than I ever did outside. No drink or drugs could give me the buzz I feel when I wake up and see the sky, rain or sunshine. There is a wonderful feeling of a private and personal linkage to something very elemental. I feel that.'

Christianity, meditation and yoga

Some people wonder how I, a Catholic nun, can practise and teach Zen meditation. I think their predicament arises from two misconceptions. One relates to the role of meditation and contemplation in the Christian tradition, and the second to the idea that meditation is linked to a particular religion rather than being a spiritual path open to all.

I was in the Orient - Japan and the Philippines - for 32 years, as a Catholic missionary. While there, my own spiritual advisors encouraged me to study under eminent Zen Buddhist Masters, who taught me the techniques of breath-focused meditation. I experienced just what they said would happen, my run-away mind became less busy, and I came to understand a fraction of that beautiful line in the Psalm, "Be still, and know that I am God."

With my Buddhist Master, there was never any problems about religion. He simply told me to continue with my Christian practices as I had always done. I love and practise contemplation in the Christian tradition which has a wonderful history. Also, speaking as a Christian trained in Zen I can surely assert, not only has there been no conflict for me, but also I feel consequently that my spirituality has been deepened and broadened by the practice of Oriental silent meditation.

In the PPT we work with inmates of any religion, Islamic, Hindu, Buddhist etc., or none, and do so in the happy knowledge that they can be helped to develop a healing spirituality through yoga and meditation. We start by developing a silent body (through yoga) and silent mind (through breath-centred meditation). Both understand the breath to be Sacred, and both employ silence. How can there be religious conflict in a silent mind?

The first book of the Bible (Genesis 2–7) states, "Then the Lord God formed man out of dust from the ground and breathed into his nostrils the breath of life and man became a living being." In other words, our breath is the breath of God. It just could be that we Christians are now in an era when we can be helped to realize how to use this precious reality.

To quote a friend and Jesuit priest, "For Christians, spirituality is nothing other than a life in attunement to the Spirit, the breath of God, wherein we let our total being be taken up in its dynamic presence. Paying attention to our breathing in yoga and meditation, is seen not simply as a physical exercise that keeps us concentrated on one point, but as the very abandonment of our total being to the breath of God, here and now."

My personal worship and religion are Christian, and I am helped along my spiritual path to the realization of the Divine by meditation. For that I am profoundly grateful. My wish is simply to help others open their door to Spiritual Reality, irrespective of their personal faiths.

Only you can know the taste.

You have to do it yourself.

A common attribute of all religions is that they are based on an experience, and they offer that experience to their adherents. So while you are sitting in your cell to help get your head straight, you are taking a definite step towards a spiritual awakening, however unwilling or unable you may be to articulate it. The important point to remember is that only you can do it, and no one else can do it for you. And the experience of meditation is like experiencing the taste of a cup of tea. You have to taste it for yourself. This is what the three inmates in Manila are telling us about their experience.

"I feel stronger as I draw all that energy, then it's used in my meditation sessions. I feel that the journey is slow and hard with many locked gates but it's not impossible and I have the keys. To me it feels true as everyone is an individual and no one can teach someone else to open those gates. It has to be learned by each individual. Tonight I was sitting in a cell playing cards when some one walked in. We got talking and I found out he writes to you too. I never said anything tonight, just took time out to listen to him. Soon, I'll say something. He's on the same line as myself and that's great."

From HMP Whitemoor

Suggested prayers before and after sitting

When I, a student of the Way, look at the real form of the universe,
All is the never-failing manifestation of the mysterious trust of What Is.
In any event, in any moment, and in any place, none can be other than the marvellous revelation of its glorious light.
This realisation made our founding meditation teachers and ancestors extend tender care, with the heart of worshipping, even to such beings as beasts and birds.
This realisation teaches us that our daily food, drink, clothes and protections of life are the warm flesh and blood, the merciful incarnation of Buddha.
Who can be ungrateful or not respectful even to senseless things, not to speak of human beings. Even though someone may be a fool, be warm and compassionate.
If by any chance such a person should turn against us, become a sworn enemy and abuse and persecute us, we should sincerely bow down with humble language,
in reverent belief that he or she is the merciful avatar of Buddha, who uses devices to emancipate us from sinful karma that has been produced and accumulated upon ourselves by our own egoistic delusion and attachment through countless cycles of kalpas.
Then on each moment's flash of our thought there will grow a lotus flower,
And on each lotus flower will be revealed a Buddha.
These Buddhas will glorify Sukhavati, the Pure Land, every moment and everywhere.
May we extend this mind over all beings so that we and the world together may attain maturity in Buddha's wisdom.

(To-rei Zenji: Bodhisattva's Vow)

***

O ALLAH...
Enlighten what is dark in me.
Strengthen what is weak in me.
Mend what is broken in me.
Bind what is bruised in me.
Heal what is sick in me.
Straighten what is crooked in me
And revive whatever peace and love has died in me...
Ameen

(Islamic Prayer)

***

Source of all being,
You created me when your purpose first unfolded.
Before the oldest of your works,
From everlasting, I was firmly set.
From the beginning before the earth came into being
The deep was not when I was born.
There were no springs to gush with water.
Before the mountains were settled
Before the hills I came to birth.
Before you made the earth, the countryside
Or the first grains of the world's dust.
When you fixed the heavens firm, I was there.
When you drew a ring on the surface of the deep,
When you thickened the clouds above,
When you fixed fast the springs of the deep,
When you assigned the seas its boundaries
And the waters will not invade the shore,
When you laid down the foundations of the earth,
I was by your side, a master craftsman,
Delighting you day after day,
Ever at play in your presence,
At play everywhere in your world,
Delighting to be with the children of the earth.

(Proverbs 8:22-31, *The Bible*)

Unseen help

Meditation practice is our daily opportunity to strengthen our sense of being more than the thinking mind. We sit down to meditate, the mind keeps trying to grab all our attention with its thoughts, and we keep re-directing our attention to the breath. The mind employs all sorts of tricks, and we fall for many of them, then we remember and return to our focal point. Gradually, if we simply persevere day in and day out, we become able to sit quietly focused on our breath, while the mind continues generating thoughts in the background. We notice most of the thoughts, but we do not get involved with them until meditation practice is over. The mind does its thing and we do ours, and we co-exist.

Every season we send out newsletters to prisoners who have been in touch with us. Each month we hold workshops in prisons all over the country. Everyday, we write to people who are captive.

When all of us at the Trust sit each morning in meditation, we hold all of you in our hearts and remember you in our prayers. Please believe that every time you practise yoga or meditation, we are with you.

Sister Elaine and Sandy

Who we are

The Prison Phoenix Trust helps prisoners turn their lives around by using their cells as places of spiritual practice. We encourage any form of healing and experience that is effective, but we ourselves concentrate on yoga and meditation. We do this through the distribution of books and articles and personal letters. We go into prisons and give workshops to prisoners and staff alike. We also give workshops to yoga and meditation teachers who wish to hold classes within UK and Irish prisons.

Meditation is the chief concern of former Director of the Trust, **Sister Elaine MacInnes**, who came to England in 1993, after spending 32 years in Japan and the Philippines as a Catholic nun. She is an accredited Zen teacher of the Sanbo Zen in Japan. After 15 years there, Sister Elaine set up a Meditation Centre for the Catholic church in the Philippines, and during the worst of the Marcos years, taught meditation to a group of political prisoners. Through the underground, they got word to Sister Elaine that they wanted a meditation teacher and, in spite of continuing hostile pressure from the authorities, she taught the prisoners meditation one day a week for four and a half years. There she was able to observe not only the therapeutic effects of this silent meditation, but also the possibility that even prisoners can come to its spiritual experience whilst incarcerated.

Yoga in prison was advanced by **Sandy Chubb**. She taught regular prison yoga classes to young offenders at HMYOI Aylesbury before setting up the Prison Phoenix Trust prison yoga teacher network. There are now more than 70 teachers offering yoga to students in prisons all over the UK. Mrs Chubb has been practising yoga for forty years and zen meditation for thirty years. She is an accreditated yoga teacher and an accredited Zen Teacher of Sanbo Zen in Japan. Until she retired as Director of the Trust in 2010, she ran workshops for adult prisoners and young offenders all over the country and encouraged prison authorities and outside teachers to offer yoga to people serving time.